# Rhapsody of the Naked Immigrants

For Linda,
Wish you endless creativity.
keep writing.

July, 2011

p.s. Happy Graduation!

# Rhapsody of the Naked Immigrants

poems by

## Elena Georgiou

Harbor Mountain Press
Brownsville, Vermont

Copyright ©2009 Elena Georgiou

Harbor Mountain Press, Inc. is a 501(c)(3) organization
dedicated to publishing works of high literary merit, with a
focus upon works of poetry.

Harbor Mountain Press appreciates the generous support
and donations from the Byrne Foundation and Pentangle
Council on the Arts.

First printing September 2009

ISBN 978-0-9815560-2-4

Series Editor:
Peter Money

Book design:
Christian Peet

Cover art:
Harley Terra Candella
Detail from "Azerbaijan", 1983
48"x52" (acrylic / canvas)
www.terracandella.com

Harbor Mountain Press
Brownsville, VT
05037

www.harbormountainpress.org

# Contents

## *public rhapsodists*

Immigrant #1: *Freedom* from Hipbone to Hipbone      5

Immigrant #2: Under a Public Skin      7

Immigrant #3: Her City's Unspoken Rule      9

Immigrant #4: Psalm of the Things She Puts Down Her Bra      10

Immigrant #5: Breaking Her City's Unspoken Rule      13

Immigrant #6: Incantation by Phone      14

Immigrant #7: Unsung Elegy      17

Immigrant #8: Blueprint of a Neck      19

Immigrant #9: Nocturne      21

Immigrants #10 & #11: Aubade for Two Lives      23

Immigrants #12 to #17: Aubade Beneath the Genius Loci      27

Immigrant #18: Prayer for an Alien with Extraordinary
Ability in the Arts      30

Immigrant #19: Song from a Fire Escape      32

## *mass in transit*

Train

STATION      37

EXPRESS      39

LOCAL      44

New York Spiritual      47

*private rhapsodist (immigrant #19)*

| | |
|---|---|
| Dream Diary of a Migrant Bird | 53 |
| Personal Ad for an Expatriate Cartographer | 54 |
| Question Air on Foreign Land | 55 |
| The Limiting Magnitude of a North American Sky | 59 |
| Psalm of the Long-Distance Beginning | 61 |
| Encomium for a One-Fold Bookbinder | 62 |
| Homeland Aubade | 64 |
| In Case of Emergency | 67 |
| Rhapsody of the Naked Lovers | 70 |
| Flamenco Confessional | 74 |

| | |
|---|---|
| *Acknowledgements* | 77 |
| *About the Author* | 79 |

*for C*

## At the Battery

I am standing on one foot
at the prow of great Manhattan
leaning forward
projecting a little into the bright harbor

If only a topographer in a helicopter
would pass over my shadow
I might be imposed forever
on the maps of this city

—Grace Paley

public rhapsodists

# Immigrant #1:
## *Freedom* from Hipbone to Hipbone

Your backpack is armor. You're alone
in New York. Your fingers lope along city blocks

drawn on the map held away from your breast—
your passport to an independent life. Your hand

on your hip and one raised eyebrow add inches to your height.
When a stranger stops to offer help, you

look him in the eye: *No.*
*Thanks. I know exactly where I'm going.*

Combat boots steering you to the New York Public Library.
Inside the stacks, you contemplate supermarkets—

how the conformity of cans increases your appetite
to read. You snake through hardbacks—Philosophy,

Astronomy, Geography, History—Egypt beckons.
Once her monarch, now only your name remains.

Was the memory of you in your kitchen of copper,
sipping rosewater, a fantasy?

Did you really ask your American guest: *How do you live,*
*alone, in a city?*

*If I'm without family for five minutes, I panic. I hate it.*
Now, you breeze down library steps,

without relatives, your city panorama mapped
in numbers and letters—grids that embrace

the pyramid of books under your arm.
You repeat the mantra you've invented:

*Each crack*
*in the pavement, the prospect of a story.*

*Each clash with a stranger, a trip closer to myself.*
Your newly-pierced nose has restored your status of royalty.

You've tattooed the word
*Freedom* from hipbone to hipbone—

permanently marking you
as a surveyor of subways. Your hair is thick clover.

Your fingernails, shovels
digging for god beneath tunnels and cement. But nothing,

not even a root offers you its flesh.
You stop on the steps,

before a clump of urban anthropologists.
You slick back your bangs, unzip your backpack:

*This,* you say, holding up a self-portrait.
*This is the history I want to display*

*at the Museum of People Who No Longer Live*
*The Lives Their Families Demand. And this,* you say,

one arm outstretched to Harlem, the other to Brooklyn,
*this is my city—home to the person I've come here to be.*

# Immigrant #2:
# Under a Public Skin

On the corner of 33rd and 5th,
         a skyline spreads silver over the skin of a Senegalese
                  taxi-driver, drunk

with fatigue and probably regret. He picks her up
         without tutting his tongue, drives towards Brooklyn.
                  The meter flicks to 2.50.

To Chinatown, between fresh fish and grime,
         past a pagoda that refuses to move
                  to a garden of tranquility, they sail

across an exhausted bridge.
         And still, after a stack of sure-footed years,
                  she cannot leave Manhattan without glancing back

to watch the colossal torsos of buildings
         shrink to less-breathtaking size.
                  Still, she cannot leave without fear

the city might disappear by morning—
         the weight of bodies
                  finally driving the slender strip of land to surrender

to quiet hours and silently sink
         into the merging Hudson and East.
                  Still, she cannot ride along Flatbush

without wanting to tap the taxi window,
         to catch a pedestrian's eye,
                  to proclaim, "This is my home."

It is a lie, of course. This is not her home.
> Her songs would be laments if she'd lived here
>> when epithets cut a girl's skin and left

a severed relationship to land.
> This land, that land, same script—*Go home.*
>> Different characters—the National Front, the Klan.

Her truth is a private graffiti
> under a public skin—
>> three countries banding together

to spray-paint: *This land is not your home.*
> *That land is not your home.*
>> *Your parents' land—*

*not home. Your only*
> *home is your hand.*
>> The meter stops at 15.00.

Like a good American, she tips generously,
> wishes the other immigrant a good night.
>> Inside her home, hungry,

she microwaves her history—
> the smells from three nations unite.
>> Tired, huddled,

her face in her hands—
> North Africa wafts from her wrist.
>> Perhaps this bit of skin could belong.

Immigrant #3:
Her City's Unspoken Rule


don't look




                                                          up

# Immigrant #4:
# Psalm of the Things She Puts Down Her Bra

She crams it with thesauruses, new ones from stores,
old ones from markets, pocket-sized dictionaries,
LPs, CDs, whatever keeps words close to her skin.

And jasmine from the trellis outside her parents' house;
the place where red dust on the veranda flies in from Libya;
the place where she says, *No, what he meant was . . .*
*No, what she was trying to say was . . .*

And if it is lacey, she tucks breezes into the left cup,
sand in the right—a holiday in her sternum;
ripples that lead to her cleavage—an island
clothed in the almond flowers of spring.

And keys, keys to her locker at the gym;
keys for offices she uses now and again;
keys to the homes of friends who interrogate life
and wait for their plants to reply.

And coins; gorgeous, green, hexagonal threepenny bits,
abandoned when twenty shillings no longer made a pound;
coins engraved with *Republic, United,* and *Great*;
quarters for laundry and phone calls to people
who have gone to *Apocalypse Now.*

And scraps of satin
she salvaged from an antique nightgown.

And the backs to earrings that fall
in the aisle.

And the earrings themselves—
intricate pairs; identical, in love,
no one accuses *them* of narcissism.

And ice cream that melts
a trail to the underwire.

And a tongue
to lick it up.

And breasts that belong
to another woman.

And a beard.

And, of course, her breasts.

And honeysuckle.

And *consider the lilies.*

And stones from New Orleans,
the Baths of Aphrodite, Aphrodite's birthplace,
Aphrodite's Rock.

And Russian dolls that grow
smaller and inside each one is a love she cannot hear
when she holds their open bodies to her ear.

And a page fragment that says:
*To understand me you have to swallow*
*a world.*

And another that says:
*Most of what matters in my life happens*
*in my absence.*

And: *Excuse me while*
*I kiss the sky.*

And if her bra is made of silk, she can't tell
the difference between a firefly, an airplane, a star;
and she crawls between the aisles
to steady herself beneath the enormousness of the sky,
where she flies with Icarus—perhaps,
together, they will not die.

And lastly, there are receipts for the sound of blue
September moons;
receipts for her camera, her cell phone, her bed;
for lovers she forgot to return;
for books she hasn't yet read;
especially this receipt for a new alarm clock
set to National Public Radio.

And the news through which she sleeps.

And the news that forces her awake.

# Immigrant #5:
# Breaking Her City's Unspoken Rule

up

my god, look

# Immigrant #6:
# Incantation by Phone

When   metal became ribbon
        & airplane tires fell
        1,000 feet from above,
when   people formed chains,
        someone flashed a light,
when   they walked out of building 5,
        I called you, Anna,
        to see if you were alive.
When   43,000 windows shattered
        & a hurricane of paper
        remained whole and flew
        to Coney Island,
        I called you, Beatrice,
        to see if you were alive.
When   some held hands
        & others grabbed shoes,
        abandoned baby
        carriages,
        I called you, Charlene.
When   some hit redial
        & said, *If I don't see you*
        *again, I love you*;
when   others called lovers
        & said, *I'm not going to make it,*
        I called you, Denise.
When   the city was struck
        dumb;
when   atheists said, *We're not*
        *religious, we don't pray,*
        *but we said a prayer*
        *to somebody, something almighty,*
        I called you, Eva.

When    someone said, *Quiet,*
        *I hear something,*
        I called you, Francesca and Greg.
When    someone asked,
        *Who did you lose?*
        I called you, Hannah.
        I called you, Isabel,
        you, Jeremiah, Keta, Lyndell.
When    the smell of smoldering
        buildings and flesh melded,
when    people wrote
        *WAR* and *GOD*
        *BLESS* in the dust, on the wind-
        shield of cars,
when    a preacher asked,
        *Is there any word from God?*
        I called you,

        Marie,
                    Nancy,

        Olaf,
                    Paul,

        Quentin,
                    Roy,

        Sharon,
                    Troy,

        Una,
                    Verna,

        Will,
                    Xianthi.

When    the BBC said, *Never
        has a city used silence
        to such eloquent effect,*

        Yin
                    &
        Zoe,
                    I called

        you.

# Immigrant #7:
# Unsung Elegy

When planes hovered over your childhood,
        hurled bombs onto the roof of your school,

your father's candy store, the post office next door,
        when your mother, father, brother, and sisters

filled four suitcases with clothes (but not photographs),
        when they fled south to be sheltered by government

tents (no stoves, no bedding,
        no remnants of dowries;

their wedding garlands buried
        beneath a heap of bedroom walls),

you weren't there.
        You were here,

where they told you to change
        your name to make you

palatable to the clientele
        who ordered avocados stuffed with shrimp,

as a ghost played jazz
        to accompany their mastication.

When planes surveyed your homeland
        scouting for more targets,

when your uncles forsook their flocks,
        your aunts abandoned their wardrobes

with their children's birthdates
        scratched into the doors,

the LPs in your living room waited,
        stacked and mute—

black vinyl tombstones,
        carved with the groove and tongue of home.

You were
        never one

to balance a water-filled glass on your head and spin
        with the poise of the boys from your village.

Instead, you sat silent—no grieving bouzouki
        to convey an elegy.

The unsung
        folded you

into the armchair you'd turned 180 degrees
        away from the coffee table, the sofa,

your daughters, your wife.
        While they faced in, you faced out,

staring beyond patio doors at preoccupied roses
        past an umbrella of crabapple trees, listening

for your ocean
        too far away to hear.

# Immigrant #8:
# Blueprint of a Neck

It started after the invasion,
after the country was broken—
one half covered in blood.

The necklaces were gold.
Silver not even a consideration.
The message: *Nothing second-rate
about our land.*

Jewelry born of division.
& necks that refused
& held the glistening whole.

I was a charlatan.
I wore it, though I could not
say: *I belong.*

My first visit, I did feel a home
in sun that drove me to discard shoes
& run in sand that burned my soles.

But I could not separate burning skin
from firearms & burning.

\*

What we inherit—jewelry, fire, skin—
nothing predicts what we will hold
in seven cervical bones.

19

\*

Since the invasion, I still run
on hot sand, & stand
up to my neck in love
for the sea.

Not *my* sea.
Not *my* sand.

& I know where I have once been
            I can no longer go.

& I did ride to the border.

& I did feel the loss of fleeing a home
            others now call their own.

& a home does not belong to the people who occupy
            the abandoned beds
            within it

but to those whose faces still hang
            in frames on derelict walls.

& yes, I left the place they came to.

& yes, I left the place I came to.

& my necklace went missing
more than thirty years ago.

But my neck still holds
the blue lines of yearning.

# Immigrant #9:
# Nocturne

It begins with last night's dream—the dilapidated
        air-raid shelter, spotlighted to look like a castle.

Is there a melancholy piano? No,
        an absurd sound for her ghetto.

Perhaps it is not melody, but memory that makes her
        body uncurl like a scroll.

The four crumbling, roofless walls
        give her what she needs—a shield.

In this shelter (this bit is real, not a dream), she is kneeling,
        her face staring into a shoebox filled with ants.

No mother calling her in for yogurt and bulgur.
        No father at home to push her solitary swing.

Silence, just silence. And ants,
        marching heroically across dandelion leaves.

Her dream contains bricks, cement, herself
        as a child. An elusive sun highlights

this ramshackle citadel.
        *Airraidshelter, airraidshelter*;

she sings it, makes it one word,
        assigns to it meaning.

(Its original one unknown to her.)
        Air raid? A raid of air?

Whatever she needs shelter from is not present.
        Besides, the roof went missing long before she arrived.

And yet, these halfhearted walls give her
        a word that does not exist in some languages—

*privacy.*
        Her *Agia Graphy.*

An ant marches across the arc of a leaf.
        Another ant crawls beneath the curve.

More ants explore the borders. Not an army, but a handful.
        Not in captivity (the shoebox has no lid),

just the temporary hostages of a child. No danger
        here, only the threat that no one will notice her for hours.

# Immigrants #10 & #11:
# Aubade for Two Lives

She loves the world
        waking up—the uncurling,

chaotic sheets;
        feet rooted on an ocean floor.

She loves the nonchalant,[1]
        the opening of the bedroom door;

the stumble to the toilet;
        the bladder's release;[2]

the first splash of water,
        the spritz, the rinse. She loves

---

[1] Dig beneath the surface of *nonchalance* to find the hum of a life that has known little ease—a newly-arrived mother without money to buy food for her eight-month-old daughter who is now sleeping more and more.

[2] The mother went to a Bushwick church and surrendered to God. His gift was milk and cheese and eggs. God was a Puerto Rican grocer. He delivered.

the amble to the kitchen;
      how the flame spreads to receive.[3]


She loves the kettle's haunches, its moan,
      its whine. She loves


the tea bag's first swim;
      its pirouette with her spoon;


the pouring, the papaya leaf,
      the rosehip, the cloves.


She loves her cup's circumference; its kiss;[4]
      her first sigh. She loves


how the bite into a grapefruit squirts juice
      in her eye. She loves


her first stretch; the first movement
      of pen; sentences, punctuation,

---

[3] God continued to drop off a cardboard box of groceries on Saturday mornings. The mother never saw him—His elusiveness began to bother her. She thought He could ring her bell to say hello. Surely, it wouldn't kill God to come in for a cup of tea.

[4] Now that her baby was fed, the mother craved a different kind of sustenance—the warmth of a lover's leg pressed against her own. In the Wyckoff Laundromat, waiting for her clothes to dry, another woman sat in the chair next to hers. As the woman parted her legs to balance the newspaper she was reading, the feel of this stranger's leg pressing against her own sucked hard at her insides.

the chance to begin
        again.


The page—she loves[5]
        how she letters it with black;


inscribes her morning
        reverie—the child


she will never have; the anniversary that is still
        a possibility. She loves[6]


her second cup of tea;
        how the china sits


by the sink, waiting,[7]
        waiting just for her.


She loves the shower—its temperamental force,
        its control, its burst. She loves

---

[5] She wanted love, not just touch. Touch, the mother knew, was easy to
come by. She could practically get it with a couple of coupons at the local
Key Food. But love was like the God who delivered her groceries—elusive.

[6] She looked for love under a cushion on her couch. She thought she'd
left a remnant there. But instead, she found a photo of her child's father.
The face made her body stiff. She tore it up to erase the memory.

[7] Waiting was something in which she had prided herself. She was not
raised in this world of the five-second soundbite. She was not a child of this
country, of this generation. Waiting, for her, was a dying art.

the first rub of towel,
          the first scratch of mat. She loves

how the day will crawl
          forward, no matter how

much of it
          she regrets.

# Immigrants #12 to #17:
# Aubade Beneath the Genius Loci

i.

He scats Rachmaninoff
       to his boyfriend[1]—his song rises

above coffee, bacon, & eggs. Sun cuts
       through glass—floods

homefries & stubble.[2]
       Love makes him break

bacon into shards & throw
       the ruins into his sweetheart's mouth.

Mozart hijacks
       the radio,[3]

---

[1] The informality of New York diners allows the City's citizens to let down their guards. In them, you can watch people with only the flimsiest of partitions between their private worlds and your own.

[2] Sundays in this City's diners are about juxtaposition—you might find someone who has just rolled out of bed, still in his stained sweatpants and wrinkled T-shirt, sitting at the table next to a person who is wearing her church hat with feathers, her pantyhose suffocating the life out of her legs.

[3] The diner here is a mix of three—one in Brooklyn Heights (where Mozart is a regular) the other in Park Slope (where James Taylor reigns), and a diner in Prospect Heights called Tom's. In Tom's, you can find a handwritten note from Suzanne Vega to Tom framed on the wall, even though Suzanne Vega was not singing about this Tom's but a Tom's in Manhattan. (Diners called Tom's abound.) This Tom's has been in existence since the '40s—the radio station still plays Glenn Miller.

but he's no match
for the lover who knocks back

his OJ, cracks
his knuckles to play

Rachmaninoff on a Formica baby
grand.


ii.
He croons Nirvana's words
(*I need an easy friend*)

to his girlfriend (*I do—
with an ear to lend*)[4]

as she bites into toast & flicks
through the *New York Times*.

She reads about women
martyrs—girls, really,

whose first pregnancies are bombs.
He scoops up his grits, drops

his croon, gulps, then sings *Come
as you are. As you were. As I want you to be.*

---

[4] It is not so easy to make friends in New York, not because of unfriendliness but because its citizens have more friends than they have time for; they are "overextended." Often, they stop responding to phone messages to lessen their number of social commitments. Here's some advice for the newcomer: 1) Expect a new friendship to take two years to form, and 2) Even though you ride the subway with hundreds of people every day, friendship seldom begins this way.

She asks him if love for a country could make him
        bandage his stomach with dynamite

& blast his body into the
        sky.


iii.

She whispers *Jesus died
        for somebody's sins*[5]

into her menu as her girlfriend orders
        Eggs Benedict & two teas. Here,

she can hold her beloved's face
        & publicly kiss her hand.

The waiter returns
        with two steaming plates. *Benedictus*

*qui venit in nominee ova,*[6] one says.
        They lean in & sing—*People say beware*[7] . . .

They raise their cups &
        sip.

---

[5] But not hers.

[6] Blessed is he that cometh in the name of eggs.

[7] New York diners are public places where lovers who share the same
gender can hold hands and not have to look over their shoulders.

29

# Immigrant #18:
## Prayer for an Alien with Extraordinary Ability in the Arts

When you are in love with your poetry
teacher and the assignment is to write
a prayer, you will want this to be
the best poem ever written. For mood,
you will take the train to a café that has porcelain ducks
floating on an ocean of wood. You will sip
mint tea; eat lemon poppyseed cake.
You will listen to Mahalia Jackson singing a spiritual, a cappella.
You will begin the freewrite with the words: Dear God of Poetry,
I am praying for the perfect prayer, a poem
to be handed from generation to generation;
studied in schools; kept by bedsides,
under pillows, on top of altars. You will want it
to have profound images, poignant metaphors,
strung together like a necklace of jet.
You will want it to sound like a hymn;
like Billie Holiday singing,
*God Bless The Child.*
You will type it up; adjust the margins;
bold the title; sign your name;
make copies; distribute it
in the workshop; read it.
There will be silence.
Two of the students will cry.
One of them will say, Wow.
The teacher will say, Well done.
She will know she has inspired great work.
She will fall in love with you too.

And then you will go on the road
to read it in cafes, in universities,
in theaters, in stadiums,
in parks, from pulpits,
at conferences, and conventions.
You will be invited to read it in Cuba.
It will be put to music and sung by a world choir.
The Pope will bless you. The Queen will knight you.
You will read it at the inauguration of a President.
And when you get to the end of the poem,
entire populations will be weeping, weeping.
You will tell them they too can write a poem like this.
They will ask you to be President. You will decline.
They will ask you to head the United Nations. You will decline.
They will name you The People's Poet. You will accept.
Only then will they give you a Green Card.

# Immigrant #19:
# Song from a Fire Escape

She wakes to *'Round Midnight* on sax. Her plants complain.
She argues her defense—*I need music*
       *like you need water.* She buys her morning
       coffee at the bodega. (There's no caffeine in her house.)
Mondays, she exercises to high-speed love
       songs that convince her
       all her decisions are right.
On the treadmill, no one sees her cry.
She conserves water;
recycles paper—*The New Yorker,*
*Harpers,* Tuesday's and Sunday's *Times.*
She uses both sides of every ream she steals.
(On one side, she prints
       the beauty of anonymity,
       on the other, the crumbling teeth in her dreams.)
Tuesdays, she lifts weights to the sound of a siren;
       sit-ups in sync with a fire engine's light.
She keeps lettuce in her fridge—a refrigerator flower—
eats it before it wilts.
Her bookcases are stacked with melancholy
       volumes that don't end
       in redemption.
(She'd add extra shelves for a lover's collection,
       should *that* need ever arise.)
There are two empty drawers in her dresser.
(They will never be filled with her clothes.)
She has hot and cold running water,
heat, and also a fan; a shower that sprays,
a toilet that flushes, tissue in constant supply.

(She hates that it's wrapped in babies' faces,
hates that they're always blonde.)
Wednesdays, kickboxing.
As she kicks she fantasizes
        she's a new superhero—
        a woman called Robin Hood
        with a primetime, syndicated show.
She believes in a Welfare State.
(She believes a country should not disown its citizens.)
She believes in Nationalized Health Care.
(She believes a country should not disown its citizens.)
She believes a woman's body belongs to the heart that drives it;
        it is utterly her own.
She believes
        in faith.
But struggles
        to sustain it.
Thursdays, she practices yoga and feels insincere chanting *Om*.
She stares at the yoga teacher's hands and wants
        the other students to disappear.
She stares at the yoga teacher's lips when she should be
        saluting the sun.
If she had souvenirs of boyfriends—a butterfly pin,
        an art deco ring—they're lost.
Her girlfriends' gifts—a water-fountain and glow-in-the-dark
        stars—are still attached to her walls.
Her fire
        escape is all the garden she needs.
Her flowers come from market.
Her kitchen floor is never dirty.
The garbage never overflows.
Fridays, she has dinner with friends.

(After midnight, trains run
		especially slow.) A Jamaican woman in transit sings
		*At last, my love has come along.*
She wishes she had a lover
		to take her laundry to the basement.
She wishes she had a lover
		to bring her black currant tea
		in bed. She has paid a woman to shape her
		brows and paint her toenails cranberry red.
The Dominican janitor takes heavy things to the basement.
A Panamanian handyman installs the AC and blinds.
Saturdays, she sees independent movies—desiccated
Tunisian widows transform into succulent bellydancers;
Moroccan chefs who succumb to recipes
for love. She's saving for the holiday of a lifetime—
		Ethiopia and then to Tibet.
		(She may never go.)
She loves roadside murals (that don't include flags)
		and broken paving stones
		where grass refuses to grow.
She's indifferent to an ex-lover
		who gave her a globe; then left her
		to wander the world alone.
She's annoyed by the one who pleads to come back—
		she employs a choir of Canadian monks
		to block her ex-lover's voice from reaching her ears.
Sundays, at dusk, she runs laps in the park—
		the city wind keeps her
		eyes dry. She turns up the syncopated
		beat of *Police & Thieves.*
She is in love with her amplified pulse and concrete
		silhouettes against sky.

mass in transit

# Train

STATION

On the steps of the subway
the artist has chalked:

*Choose     Love*
My right foot steps on *Choose.*

My left on *Love.*
Inside the station, a sign:

> No begging
> for an ear

> No sharing
> your isolation

> No telling
> how you spent your weekend

in your apartment,
silent & alone.

As the train screeches in the tunnel,
a woman hurtles down the steps behind me

chanting, *Jesus*—
I lodge my foot in the closing doors—*Jesus.*

Her body forces its way in.
*Thank you,* she sputters. *Thank you,*

*Lord.* & though this is not the last train on Earth,
she is grateful to me, & her God.

EXPRESS

Eastern Parkway—

When the train heaves out of the station,
no matter how crowded the cars, it sings,

*There's a place for us.* Inside, there's space
for the families in our groins, the tribes in our bones.

& though our surnames are not labels
sewn onto the sleeves of our coats,

we know each other by our hustle,
our promise, posture, & might.

Grand Army Plaza—

                                        On our train,
Earth is cut in half, its crust scooped out—
the yarmulke fitted to that pale boy's head.

                                        On our train,

Africa is leather—
a continent sprawls across that man's chest.

                                        On our train,

a woman without shoes speaks
to our reflections, arrested in glass:

*Suppose I set you all free . . .*
Our silence deepens—

some of us contemplate
her call.

Bergen Street—

What emancipation
would we choose?

You, would you empty your briefcase,
toss those manuscripts into the river,

peel off your hose, run barefoot,
as far as you can, west?

You over there, would you remove your tongue
from your boyfriend's mouth, switch

from attitude to mansuetude—
a parson's wife in a tiny town?

Would I swap my view of the Chrysler spire
for six rolling acres at Copake Falls?

Atlantic Avenue—

You, would you turn your hat to the front,
buy a fiddle & let it lead you to a bluegrass South?

And you, would you refuse to erect steel girders,
& say farewell to a fragmented sky?

You in the corner, the alphabet on your knees,
as your child recites A is for Algonquin,

B is for Blackfoot. . . , is your mind drifting
to Delaware, or anywhere away from this car?

& me? Would I flee five-borough crowds
at Sakura Matsuri

or stand under Brooklyn cherry blossoms
banging a Taiko drum?

Nevins Street—

*For the east side line,*
*change here.*

Inside each commuter are two passengers—
one of words & one of wordlessness.

The passenger of words says: *Could you move*
*further inside? Excuse me. Could you move your bag?*

The passenger of wordlessness thinks:
*Why am I alone?*

When what I know about love evaporates,
a question is born in an aperture of doubt:

Is anonymity the reason for only one
empty cup in my sink?

I squeeze my doubt between two filled seats.
The man on my right bangs closed his legs.

The man on my left refuses
to make his knees touch.

Borough Hall—

Headlines leap
towards my gut:

*DRUNK DRIVER KILLS FAMILY OF THREE*
*AND UNBORN CHILD*

*BODY FOUND*
*IN RIVER*

*BEAUTY*
*SLAIN*

Words roll & hit.
I continue to ride.

Bowling Green—

A mother re-braids her child's hair; the child rests her cheek
on her lap. *The train is like a ride,*

*Mommy. The train is like a ride.*
She opens her book: *Meeting the Mohicans.*

Her mother returns to reading *The Hudson:*
*The River That Flows Both Ways.*

The train streams in, doors slide open:
*Für Elise* fills the platform—

Beethoven enters, bequeathing to the Trinidadian
a solitary steel drum.

Wall Street—

*If you see*
*a suspicious package . . .*

To those with seats,
the car is an assembly line of crotches.

*. . . do not keep it to yourself.*
*Please notify an MTA employee immediately.*

Two men enter with a map in their hands,
French in their mouths,

*Where are you trying to get to?*
asks an American.

*Paris, France,*
answers one of the French.

Crotches tremble.
A man with a graveyard on his chest translates:

*Where are you trying to get to?*
*Not: Where are you from?*

Fulton Street—

The train slides to a stop,
the open doors usher in

a burgundy-suited Jamaican preacher:
*The devil will tell you... the devil will say ...*

*but when you have the name of the Lord*
*on your tongue, your life will shine.*

A man enters with fishing rods & nets.
A woman enters, playing a fugue on her comb.

Today, like every day, is high & holy—
passengers gathered

in a peripatetic temple
to ride.

Brooklyn Bridge—

*For the local train,*
*change here.*

43

## LOCAL

Inside this un-air-conditioned car,
it's just me and a militia of orange

plastic. I tilt back my head
to keep tears in place.

Fluorescent lights flood my face—
on mass transit even tears look ugly.

On he gets—the man
with curly black hair & a notebook.

Rapt in his writing,
he sweeps the page while I hide

behind *Leaves of Grass.* Trapped
inside his curls is a tiny, white flower.

A voice tells us: *We are being held,
momentarily, by the train dispatcher.*

"Excuse me," I say, "you've something in your hair."
I pick it out. Hand it to him, "It's a flower."

"Ah, sí, I was reading. In the wind. In the park.
Were you crying . . . "

(This newcomer has not yet learned subway etiquette—
when a stranger weeps, it's merciful not to notice.)

"No," I say, shocked. "Yes," I surrender.
"Why do you bring your sorrow on the train?"

"Sorrow," I say, "is not something I carry;
it's something, unspoken, lodged in my heart."

He stares at the flower lost in his palm,
peers into its petals as if reading my future.

"I know who you are." (I recognized his face.)
"Didn't the Fascists kill you in Granada?"

"My body?
Yes, they killed it.

But, my soul," he says, "divides its time
between Andalucia and New York."

"May I read, for you?" He stands
(& does not wait for my answer).

"Mi poema:"
(The blossom drops.)


### Ode To A Love Affair That Has Not Yet Begun

*Jump in your car & drive to me, drive to me.*

    *Put rocks on your poems so they don't fly away.*

        *Pitch your tent at a site called Beginning.*

    *Wake up & salute a consummate sun.*

*Jump in your car & drive to me, drive to me.*

*Put rocks on your poems so they don't fly away.*

*Prodigal poet, reach me besotted.*

*Soon-to-be lover, bathe me in wet.*

*Newest inhabitant, discard your car,*

*pass through the turnstile & enter*

*this subterranean throng.*


Local slows
to meet Express.

Grand Central—

*Please remember*
*your personal longings.*

# New York Spiritual

Praise the rivers, the urban ripples,
city waves,
lines on the sidewalk
that make the houses fall, your mother die.
Praise skyscrapers
for piercing tough clouds.
Praise trees for reaching to an oblivious sky.
Praise the rush hours,
digs in the back,
protruding knapsacks.
Praise the closing doors,
the conductor's indecipherable voice,
the yellow line
on the platforms,
the tracks, the rats.
                    Praise, praise the subways.
Praise the workplace,
the phones, the fax,
the copy machines,
the copy machines,
the copy machines.
Praise email, the internet.
And all thanks and
praises to the computer,
the C drive, the A drive.
Praise spellcheck.
Praise the public
libraries and cafes.
And okay, praise the poetry
readings, the unending open mics,

the outrageous slams.
Praise also the universities,
the teachers, the students, the psychic readers,
the synagogues, the mosques, the churches,
the temples and tattoo parlors.
                    Praise the decorated and the devout.
Praise the fourth generation, third generation,
second and first.
Praise the natives,
the recent,
the tenants,
the apartment buildings,
the rents,
the walk-ups,
the elevators,
the doormen,
the stoops,
the soup kitchens, shelters,
the homeless, the Vets. Praise
the cabbies, yellow taxis,
their horns, their brakes.
Praise the murals
and streetlamp mosaics.
                    Praise, praise the struggling grass.
Praise the lack of solitude,
lack of space. Praise
New Yorkers who are up in your face.
Praise the sincerity of our distrust.
the keys in our hands,
our wallets buried deep,
        eyes lowered to the street.
Praise each syllable uttered

into each cell phone. Also
praise vegan restaurants
that do not allow cell phone use.
Praise all restaurants—Italian,
Mexican, Polish, Thai, Japanese,
Chinese, Indian, Cuban, Cuban-Chinese.
      And praise all the delis.
      And praise all the diners,
jukeboxes, beat boxes, djimbes,
upside down plastic buckets.
Praise noise.
Praise spit.
Praise the sidewalk—each elbow bumped,
each shoulder hunched, each twist
in every naked tree.
            Praise, praise the sex shops.
Praise hotdogs,
Praise pretzels,
the glorious knish.


      And thanks and praises to all the street vendors.
      And hallelujah and praises to all the bodegas.


Praise the opinionated, the performers,
the crusaders, the pontificators,
the dowdy, the divas, the dregs,
the runaways, the fabulous,
the anonymous, the underdressed rich,
the overdressed poor, the overentitled,
the underrepresented, the coupled,
      and, oh yes, the single.

Praise the recovering, the preachers,
the therapists, the artists,
the writers,
the writers,
the writers,
the writers,
the West Village,
East Village,
downtown
and up.

                    Praise, praise the skyline.

And
I just can't stop
praising the skyline. I

just can't stop
praising the skyline. I

just can't stop
praising the sky line—

New York.

private rhapsodist
(immigrant #19)

# Dream Diary of a Migrant Bird

I was flying in an unfamiliar rain while shouting a Cuban bolero that should have been whispered or at least chirped. An oversized umbrella made out of a rainbow covered my shouts. I asked my dream why my shouts were holding an umbrella. The dream responded, Because a bolero needs a rainbow to cover it. & because it rains in New York more than it does in Cuba. I hear the sound of wet. The radio is waving *Ribbon in the Sky*. I close my eyes and imagine what it would be like to be blind, walking along sand in Havana. The blackness my eyelids creates is soft, satiny, immaculate. Snow. They've predicted it for today. If I were blind I would not see New York snow. If I were blind I would not see Cuban sand. And it would be much harder to fly. I spent yesterday studying syntax. An owl asked, How are you? Lost in English sentences & yearning for Spanish lyrics, I answered. I'm trying to map my journey on paper. What am I going to do with my life? Fly north? Fly south? I want to write about love but instead I fly—beating, repeating the movement of my pen. There is a hole in my body I'm trying to fill up. There is a spreading palmetto with a broken branch that keeps snapping with each flap of my wings. There is a tall pine with branches beckoning me to sit & sing. Time to enter the war zone, I said. Time to find love. I flew out of the city and found a Zapata Rail with her orange legs perched on a closed parenthesis of moon. She sang:

*Two little birds*
*Sitting on a moon*
*One named paper*
*One named pen*
*Fly away paper*
*Fly away pen*
*Come back love*
*Come back wings*

)

# Personal Ad for an Expatriate Cartographer

*Seeking:* a self-educated lover         of words that end
with an L, especially *daffodil,*     *sensual,* and *windowsill;*
a punctual perambulator  willing to meander
across my stomach to create             desire lines in skin
as well as the ones             we will create
together         in  Prospect Park.

*Wanted:* a person who will kiss my wrists  in a cornflower field;
who has already leapt    into a Hudson River of books;
who has been hypnotized by East River clouds,     and regrets
the human        appropriation of sky;

who wants exiled silk worms             to build cozy cocoons;
who employs owls        as tutors          on how to thread
a needle             on the subway         at night.

*Please:* no one who rolls suitcases            inside cigarette paper;
douses their cereal with Arrack or Rum;    no one
who does not worship             the rebellion of an urban star
& the folly in the uni-    verse of an expatriate cartographer
attempting to map the randomness of love.

# Question Air on Foreign Land

*Do you remember the first time you fell in love?*

Yes, wordless, standing inside an Ambassador's door.
Sitting cross-legged on an American Embassy's floor.

I saw two deer behind eyes.
I looked away.

They told me they were galloping from London to Paris.
When they got to France, they thought Paris would be right there.

I waited until the deer returned.
My voice was low.

African. American. A whisperer.
Hyphens existed between continents and sounds.


*When you feel an attraction, which parts of the body catch your eye?*
*(10 corresponds to the most attractive feature, 1 to the least):*

|               | 1 | 2 | 3 | 4 | 5 | 6 | 7 | 8 | 9 | 10 |
|---------------|---|---|---|---|---|---|---|---|---|----|
| Eyes          |   |   |   |   |   |   |   |   | x |    |
| Hair          |   |   |   |   |   |   |   |   | x |    |
| Neck          |   |   |   |   |   | x |   |   |   |    |
| Legs          |   |   |   | x |   |   |   |   |   |    |
| Shoulders     |   |   |   |   | x |   |   |   |   |    |
| Back          |   |   |   |   |   | x |   |   |   |    |
| Teeth         | x |   |   |   |   |   |   |   |   |    |
| Lips          |   |   |   |   |   |   | x |   |   |    |
| Chest/breasts |   |   |   |   |   | x/x |  |   |   |    |
| Belly         |   |   |   |   | x |   |   |   |   |    |
| Feet          |   |   |   |   | x |   |   |   |   |    |
| Hands         |   |   |   |   |   |   |   |   | x |    |
| Skin          |   |   |   |   |   | x |   |   |   |    |

*What was the person like?*
(*Describe physical features and personality*)

Inside hair follicles were songs about lions.
        Arms carried cowries away from the shore.

I had to lean close to hear.
        I gave thanks for whispering.

Hyphenated bodies united.
        We found the courage to enter the Atlantic & swim.


*If you are in love now, circle the symptoms you display:*

o       A jalopy becomes a transcendent chariot.

o       Telephones become instruments of love.

o       You leave the city to build a stone house in the wilderness.

o       War feels distant.

o       Time is concurrently urgent and unimportant.

o       Tears become a tangible representation of God.

o       Poverty feels simultaneously real and unreal.

o       You can't eat.

o       You discover a portal that leads to a new alphabet.

o       You can't sleep.


I circled them all.

*Similes:  Love is like . . .*

| | |
|---|---|
| *an element of nature* | snow |
| *a geographical area* | a canyon |
| *a season of the year* | autumn |
| *food or drink* | watermelon juice |
| *furniture* | a chest of drawers |
| *an animal* | a seahorse |
| a plant | a vine |

*Use your ideas to create a love poem.*

*If you expressed your feelings, how did you do so?*
*If not, why not?*

I did not. I could not—Ghanaian gold adorned one finger.
    *Some Enchanted Evening* was experience, not song.

But my telephone kept making me dial the number.
When the phone rang, I counted the rings before I hung up.


**When Love Happens**

    cut watermelon

    into a canyon of snow

    melt red     collect it

    in drawers     in chests

    autumnal seahorses

weave    umbilical vines—

a botanical net

—we're caught.


We traveled across borders—lines, angles, curves.
We studied the geometry of our knees.

# The Limiting Magnitude of a North American Sky

You stand outside at 1 a.m. clutching coffee;
its steam, a smoke signal to your face.

You look into the canyon, even in darkness,
the thousand-foot drop does not scare you.

On your night-hike of Bryce, you inch to its edge,
convinced this planet will catch you if you fall.

                    And from my illuminated city,
                    I sing:


Tell me of your moonless sky, those 11,000 stars—
the perpetual opening of windows.

Tell me how you dream of a new constellation—
the cow-gut and tortoise shell of lyre

replaced with the baby goat that pulls
the l, o, v, e of adulterating light.

Tell me how a black sky has ever endured
as long as this naming.


                    No. Don't.


Tell me, instead, about worship;
how you pray to the Milky Way—

a cathedral glinting on your pastoral horizon. Console me,
for the handful of squinting stars I see from my stoop.

Ask me to visit, to witness your galaxy of mountains,
the shining of Jupiter (Optimus Maximus), you.

Promise me devotion as old as the Grand Staircase,
as ancient as pink sand dunes and Bristlecone Pine.

Tell me you want me with you at midnight
inside a Ponderosa desert—

black, unpolluted by light.

# Psalm of the Long-Distance Beginning

And you are tangled, the untamed heath
        sprawling across the city of my birth.

And your hands are trees—
        my elms, your palms.

And you keep your side of the world awake
        by drumming on skin.

And while I dream of deified weeds,
        you invoke organic terrains in ink.

And you send me your enclosed everything.

And I am not there to watch your hair grow.

And our hair is long.

And we braid our distance.

And within a curl of cross-country sighs
        we agree to meet amid expectant grass.

And our cord is concealed.
        But our connection cloudless.

And I stray into your prominent sky.

And you stumble into my valiant skyline.

And since our language has only one root,
        our private world, one map,

you find me at the end of this line.

# Encomium for a One-Fold Bookbinder

One simple fold and you create a mountain peak—
a valley turned over; a world un-spinning,

un-round; its flatness delineates where one page ends,
another begins. You are grateful for its edges—

a continuous coastline; new shores on which to write
your terrain. Here life swells into an arc—

a four-movement orchestration—
paper, hands, words, thread.

\*


One simple fold and you taught me to be
vigilant—to move the cup away from my elbow

when making the bed; to focus on your back
when entering our home, to revere your thumb,

the angle at which you hold the awl.
(In your hands "pierce" becomes a tender verb.)

\*


Dear Newly-Arrived Bookbinder,

Gather
        your hand-cut stacks of paper.

Thread
      the needle with Canadian hemp.

Hand-
bind two lives—one fold.

# Homeland Aubade

Iraq a footnote
       to the news of flus & clones

as I squeeze a ruffle of white mint
       paste onto a spine of clear bristles,

part my lips, & lift the brush
       up, down, & around.[1]

In our bedroom, you sweep
       aside a handmade heart

to clear space for your tree-hugger cup.
       (You are far from home.)[2]

My teeth know the drill—front, then left,
       then right. Then again, left, right.

You turn our pillows upright to support
       the length of our backs,

---

[1] Plaque: an inscription on a hard surface—a goodbye: *To General X for loyal service to your country.*

[2] Uprooted from 20 acres of forest & dragged to three adjoining concrete boxes, four flights up. This cup reminds you this urban dwelling is temporary. Soon, we will live among Paperbark Maples, Atlas Cedars, & in the company of Black Oaks.

prop them against the headboard—
      guards standing vigil.[3]


I spit out the paste, unroll the green
      floss, cut it to size. I lower it


between each tooth, slide it backwards,
      forwards, & wrap it around.


You move to your computer
      to scan early-morning emails—


an invitation to a wedding,[4]
      & poems from an American soldier.[5]


My pajama sleeves are damp
      with maps of silk countries—


territories that span from my elbows to my hands.
      You read the soldier's words:


"Babylon Toyotas", "frigidity,"
      "pornography," & "air." [6]

---

[3] UN peacekeepers with non-threatening, light-blue berets. But even these berets sit on top of razor-sharp haircuts worn by men holding rifles.

[4] From an ex-lover—*The bell invites me. / Hear it not, Duncan; for it is a knell / That summons thee to heaven or to hell.*

[5] Benjamin Buchholz

[6] From Buchholz's "Mailcall"

My mouth is ready for the coffee
         you've poured into a ladybird

cup, & placed on a doily
         crocheted by my refugee aunt.[7]

You leave your screen, return to bed.
         We toast the day

with full American cups.  The soldier's words drift back
         as you drink—"Babylon Toyotas" & "air."[8]

Each morning, my vista is the same—
         you outlined in gold-leaf;

beyond, an expanse of leaves—
         a fan of open arms.[9]

---

[7] She fled her home in '74 when an army invaded & claimed her land. You can still see the blue berets of UN troops pacing along barbed wire, divided land.

[8] Later, you send him an email saying you wish he could send himself home as an attachment.

[9] Flesh, that is, not guns.

# In Case of Emergency

As I fly
you track my flight
follow online circles that show
me soaring above JFK
until the fuel runs low.
You watch me re-routed to VT.
Convinced my plane did not touch
down in Burlington,
but, rather, was knocked
out of the sky
by lightning, tossed
toward earth
by a tornado, you curse
the god of inclement
weather that has intruded
to take me from you.

As if I would go.
I would not.
I would resist god.
I would say: No,
I will not step silent
into a makeshift grave,
a premature night.

I will not allow my body
to plummet past clouds,
to be buried
under a pile of broken wings,
fuselage, & snow.
I will not go. Not now. No.

For you, I push my carry-on luggage under my seat,
& turn off my ipod, my cell phone, & all portable electrical devices.
For you, I keep my seatbelt fastened, my table restored,
my seat upright.
For you, I sit by the emergency exit, prepared
to cover my nose with an oxygen mask,
& locate my vest.
&, if necessary, use my seat cushion as a flotation device.
For you, I am prepared to push, to shove, to pull, turn,
or otherwise open the emergency exit.
For you, I jump
into the sky.
Fall to snow.
For you, I packed a waterproof tarp, two blankets stored
in a plastic bag, a first aid kit in a weatherproof carton, & splint.
For you, I made my rescue plan, packed a pencil,
& two short-handled shovels.
For you, I dressed warmly, packed a loud-hailer, a rescue whistle,
& a warning horn.
For you, I packed a flagging vest with my own Avalanche Rescue
crest—an arc of gold embroidery that says:

SUGAR ON SNOW

For you, I packed a roll of red flagging tape, thirty bamboo
marking wands in green, orange, & blue,
tied the tape to each to mark the avalanche deposit, but not
the boundary of love.
For you, I packed four headlamps, a hand lantern,
five Cyalume lights, four 100-foot ropes, three pairs of snowshoes,
& a toboggan kit.
For you, I land in a pink plastic sled salvaged from a dump.

For you, I hold the rope as a reign, steer myself down
a snow-covered hillside, carving a path.
  Screaming, I bump into your feet.
  Alight on my stomach. For you,
  my mouth is open. For you,

I kiss qanisqineq. For you,

I kiss muruaneq.

nutaryuk

qanuk

kaneq

natquik. For you,

I kiss aniu.[1]

---

[1] Yupik words for snow floating on water, for soft deep snow, for fresh
snow, for snowflake, for frost, for drifting snow, for snow on ground.
These words are from the Central Alaskan Yupik language. It is spoken by
about 13,000 people in the coast and river areas of Southwestern Alaska
from Norton Sound to Bristol Bay.

## Rhapsody of the Naked Lovers

What is at stake?  One word: *Love.*

But this is not enough. If this is about love then I need to invite everyone to join me.

And so I do. I invite you. All.

I offer these words:

> You rise from midnight swings & take me
> to your own personal forest.

> You spread Indian cloth to make a bed
> on your own personal grass.

And though this forest and this grass were once personal they now belong to everyone.

And though these are not *the saddest lines.* And I have not said, *The night is starry / and the stars are blue and shiver in the distance . . .*

I, too, want an audience to spontaneously rise to recite:

> You offer me alfalfa & clover,
> sky, & your own personal stars.

> Together we worship July Catherine Wheels—
> a tie-dyed rapture in your own personal sky.

And though these stars and this sky were once personal they are now communal.

*Forest, grass, stars,* and *sky* strip us to our skin.

Naked, we say:

> You lay your lips on mine,
> > we are united inside a lattice of hair.

> We move seamlessly—
> > from small talk to prayer.

Naked, we say:

Some of us refuse to make a public promise of commitment—
to the exclusion of all others. Instead we join, *en masse,* to

> move seamlessly—
> > from small talk to prayer.

For some lovers, wedlock means they are less likely to walk
away if love does not mature in the manner they'd anticipated.

Instead of leaving after five years, they stay until ten, perhaps
even twenty. And the day they leave is the day they cannot
imagine staying one minute longer.

For other lovers, marriage means forever.

But some of us do not want this knot because of a history of
knots that left no space for the wedded one to dream.

Instead, we make our commitment daily, upon waking. We
take our cups to the window and walk the horizon.

This line leads us further into the dream of

> moving seamlessly—
> > from small talk to prayer.

One lover says: My body is a shell that has lost its ocean and this loss makes me panic when you are not by my side. When you smell the sea, lead me toward it, place me in it, I am calm and the singing inside me begins again.

Another lover says: I am a crab without you—I walk sideways, hiding in holes, deaf to all music.

But instead of writing about walking sideways and hiding in holes in silence, on behalf of all lovers, I write:

> You lay your lips on mine,
> > we are united inside a lattice of hair.

And these words move us to Carnegie Hall.

And to ensure that all who want to be in the audience are with us, free tickets are given out at the entrance to subway stations.

Lovers are offered tickets in Caribbean Brooklyn, Chinatown, Latin-American Harlem, and Asian-American Queens.

Lovers are offered tickets in Middle Eastern Queens, Hasidic, Russian, and Haitian Brooklyn, Little Italy, and African Harlem.

Tickets even reach the multitudinous ethnicities of Staten Island lovers because someone had the foresight to hand them out at the ferry's exit.

And because we're not sure where the largest group of Native lovers has clustered, a Representative of Love is sent to the Native American Community House to invite the lovers there (who do not need tickets, since this is their home) to join us.

When all the seats in the concert hall are full, the audience chants: Recite "Rhapsody of the Naked Lovers." But I cannot remember my words.

Then the audience stands, as one, and begins:

> You rise from midnight swings & take me
> to your own personal forest.

> You spread Indian cloth to make a bed
> on your own personal grass.

(*I join in*)

> You offer me alfalfa & clover,
> sky, & your own personal stars.

> Together we worship July Catherine Wheels—
> a tie-dyed rapture in your own personal sky.

> You lay your lips on mine,
> we are united inside a lattice of hair.

> We move seamlessly—
> from small talk to prayer.

And we are all here. Close.

If only we always moved seamlessly.

# Flamenco Confessional

Forgive me, for I have raised my hands over my head,
flicked my wrists, stamped my feet, & taunted

the audience in my livingroom that applauds,
screams, & jumps to its feet,

to demand more every time Paco de Lucia plucks
notes that blossom from his strings.

Forgive me, for I have coveted the voice of a Spanish balladeer
who mines every note of yearning

buried beneath the sound of acoustic guitar.
& when the children's choir joins the chorus

I have shamelessly edged my way to the front
to stand in the line of her vision,

to be the one she sings to when the music stops.
Forgive me, for I am jealous of the musical pause—

an aphrodisiac of expectation,
followed by a slap of wood,

a hand against a hip of guitar.
Forgive me, for my hips have made love to missionaries—

upright mini-gods who converted me
to all the religions the world has to offer.

For I spun them on my fingertips, transformed them
into dervishes whirling to our erogenous dawns.

For after 1001 sunrises, I left them weeping
at the sweet withdrawal of breast.

Forgive me, for I have lain with your daughter
in snow-coated fields & swallowed the heat in her mouth.

For we kissed until our mattress melted
& the grass gave us thanks.

Forgive me, for I have also lain with your son
while two gray stallions carried us across an Arabian sky;

while we pretended we understood the words
to a language written under my chin.

Forgive me, for I have learned every scream goes both ways—
death, lament, birth, praise.

For I have crawled inside a glorious god, stolen a rib,
& created a lover who carries home pomegranate juice

in a blue & white cup from the corner bodega
to make a paper Parthenon into an origami heaven,

while an urban deity
clicks castanets by my eye.

# Acknowledgements

My deepest gratitude is extended towards the poets with whom I've shared intimate and inspiring conversations over generous slices of Blood Orange Cake: Jan Clausen, Beatrix Gates, Joan Larkin, and Steve Turtell. Thanks, also, to Debora Lidov, Marie-Alyce Devieux, and Lauren Sanders for their comments on earlier versions of this book. I would also like to thank the Virginia Center for the Arts for offering me the space to write.

I taught undergraduate poetry for many years in various colleges of the City University of New York (CUNY). What I noticed during that time was that every semester at least one student would write a poem about the subway—so, thank you, to the NYC subway and to CUNY undergrads for all they inspired.

Thank you, also, to Peter Money and Harbor Mountain Press for their enthusiasm and support. And thank you to Caroline Ashby for all that she has offered to refine this book.

And finally, thank you to Christian Peet, who turned up the volume until I could hear life sing.

Grateful acknowledgement is made to the editors of the following journals in which versions of these poems have appeared: "Flamenco Confessional" and "Immigrant#1: Freedom From Hipbone to Hipbone," *Bloom*; "Immigrant #8: Under A Public Skin" and "Immigrant #9: Incantation (By Phone)," *BOMB Magazine*; "New York Spiritual," *The*

*Cream City Review*; "Immigrant #3: Elegy" and "Immigrants #5 & #6: Aubade For Two Lives," *MiPoesias*; "Immigrant #16: Song From A Fire Escape," *Lumina*; "Question Air On Foreign Land" and "Immigrant #2: Psalm Of The Things She Puts Down Her Bra," *Tarpaulin Sky*.

I would also like to thank Amber McMillan at The Center for Book Arts, who made a broadside out of "Under A Public Skin." And thanks also to Randall Woolf from the Composers Collaborative, who created a musical hybrid from the words of two of my poems, "Song from a Fire Escape" and "Psalm of the Long-Distance Beginning."

# About the Author

Elena Georgiou is the author of *mercy mercy me*, which won a Lambda Literary Award for poetry, was a finalist for the Publishing Triangle Award, and was reissued by the University of Wisconsin Press in 2003. She is also co-editor (with Michael Lassell) of the poetry anthology, *The World In Us* (St. Martin's Press). Georgiou has won an Astraea Emerging Writers Award, a New York Foundation of the Arts Fellowship, and was a fellow at the Virginia Center for the Creative Arts. She is a member of the faculty in the MFA program at Goddard College, Vermont.